THE OLD MANDARIN

THE OLD

MANDARIN

MORE TRANSLATIONS FROM THE CHINESE

by Christopher ^Darlington Morley

With Illustrations by Carl Rose

*"So you won't need to cancel
The thoughts that you really
think,
Use less indelible pencil
And more invisible ink."*

HARCOURT, BRACE AND COMPANY   1947

LOGAN PEARSALL SMITH

1865-1946

One master of diminutive
  In an expansive generation
Learned how long an art can live
  By condensation.

None of these Translations have been collected in book form before. Many are reprinted, with due acknowledgment, from The Atlantic, The New York Times, The Saturday Review of Literature, *and* The Commonweal. *In* The Commonweal *several of them masqueraded under the temporary title "Poems on Postcards." Two were in* The Chicago Daily News.

If a complete codex of the "Translations from the Chinese" were desired, it could be found in the following volumes:—

And in "C. M.'s Briefcase," published by J. B. Lippincott Company in 1936, is a series of "Translations from the South American," probably as Chinese as the others.

C. M.

Roslyn Heights, L. I.
November, 1946

INDEX OF FIRST LINES

1

PREFACE

Anything here said or suggested,
Any likeness to actual human beings
(Drunk or sober, dead or alive)
Is, I hope, intentional.

2

THOUGHT WHILE DRESSING

Minds are like socks:
Wear them sometimes inside-out
So the holes
Come in different places.

3

PHILOSOPHER

Fun and games!
Confucius claims
That he knows nothing about dames.
He says: "Damn if I'd
Take up a subject that's so ramified."

4

ROMANCE

You thought New York architects
Are not romantic?

You see those phony gargoyles
Thirty storeys aloft,
Humbugs on the sky.

They watch over Poo Pitty Sing's
Bank account
In the basement.

5

DOUBLETAPH

I hated to see him die,
But he couldn't eat Prune Pie.

Nor, as a matter of fact, could I.

BAUBLE FOR CRITICS

I am weary
Of critical theory.

I'm empiric
About a lyric.

Either it sings
Like a happy peasant,
Or—one of those things—
It just doesn't.

7

CHINESE SONNETEER

I've only got the last line, but the rest
    Will come, I hope, eventual, late or soon;
And this will be the climax and the best:—
    The low, large, red, refracted rising moon.

CONDITIONED

Your civilization is conditioned to horror.
The roar and rocking of a commuters' train
In the Long Island tunnel,
Or the mob in Times Square on New Year's Eve,
Would cause a simple coolie
Or even a dog of unspoiled nerves
To brace himself aghast.

Little old ladies riding to town for shopping
Accept it as perfectly normal.

9

DEDICATION

I am dedicated to the proposition
To be busy is not all man's mission.
He can also serve his nation
By intervals of cerebration.

This may be envy, affectation,
Sloth, or self-justification—
Gee whiz,
Most everything is.

JITTERS

It's really serious, said the Old Mandarin.
I'm so pooped
That if no one else interrupts me
I interrupt myself.

DAPPER DAN

My bowl is caked,
My stem is clogged,
My mixture is a nicotiner—

Run me through
And dredge the goo
With your woolliest pipe-cleaner.

12

G.B.S., 1856—

What obsequies for dear old Shaw
Who lived outside the canon law?
Let's give him, to be truly Shavian,
All rites, including Scandinavian.

13

DEMI-PAX

History, impartial and empiric,
    Pays off, in average, as man deserves:
We have, for being weary and hysteric,
    Pax neurotica; the Peace of Nerves.

14

POKER FACE

ENERGY, when interviewed,
Men's anxiety pooh-poohed:—

I'm not going to beat my gums
    If they do it their or *my* way—
They can perish wholesale by atom bombs,
    Or, retail, on the highway.

15

THE DRIP

See the blisters on the manuscript
(Cried the sentimental collector)
Where the poet wept
With love and self-pity!

Bosh, said Sung Lo
(A rival poet),
It was just his messy habit
Of making notes in the bathtub.

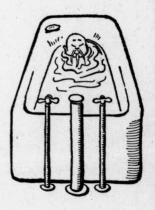

16

CLINIC

I visited a friend
In a swanky hospital.
Briskly turning a corridor
I fell heavily on the waxed pavement.
"Thrombosis!" I screamed
To the costly receptionist:
"I've fallen on your antiseptic terrazzo
And broken my rickets."

The greatest danger in a modern hospital
Is not the surgeon's knife
Nor the sprightly nurse
But the slippery floors.

ITALICS THEIRS

I overheard two lady drinkers
    Confiding at a bar:
"You mustn't think *all* men are stinkers—
    That is, not more than they *are*."

TWO OLD FRIENDS

The tiresome old Chancellor
Was boring the Duchess:
"I'm worried about my daughter,
Such a lovely girl,
But terribly frustrated."

The Duchess
(Who had just been to the frigidaire
To fetch out a snort)
Replied bluntly, "If she's as sweet as you say,
Why doesn't somebody
Defrust her?"

19

FUEL RATION

If the house is too cold
Put on dark glasses
And feel warmer at once.
It makes everything look like
Thunder weather.

20

FOURTH WEEK IN MAY

Blanche, the dogwood, casts her silver. Tragic!
Brune, the thrush, is wheedling bedtime. Magic!
And only I, in habit pedagogic,
Keep demanding: Logic . . . Logic? . . . Logic!

21

D-DAY PLUS X

Never write up a diary
On the Day itself.
It needs longer than that
To know what happened.

22

ALMANAC

On a calendar, F.M. means Full Moon;
On a radio program, Frequency Modulation;
But the idea is the same.
Who modulates frequencies
So graciously as she?

O swear not, Juliet might have said,
By the Frequency Modulation.

RASPBERRY

How sore the children were:
Every speaker at Junior High
Invariably said,
"Our generation made a mess of things,
Now it's up to You Young People
To do better."

Only the presence of the faculty
Prevented those indignant scholars from shouting:
"Balloons! Take a powder!
Get the high-tail out of here!"

COFFEE AFTER DINNER

Formosa's legs twice justify
Her dress's trick of riding high,

But from those charms her words detract—
Her mind, poor dear, is vacuum-packed.

UNCONSCIOUS FELICITY

Often imperfect in American idiom
The O.M. amuses his students:
Work hard, my dears, he advises;
Keep your nose to the groundstone.

26

LOOKING FOR THE SWATTER

Nothing is trivial:
One bluebottle fly
Touring aimlessly round the ceiling
Can prevent a whole poem
From being written.

27

THE MAINSPRING

I know what keeps people going.
It's the thought everyone sometimes has:
"Wouldn't it be wonderful
If I weren't actually as stupid
As I know I really am."

TOO LATE

The fountain pen I used so long
Touched by a burning cigarette
Sizzled away in white camphory smoke.
I had never guessed
It was so inflammable.

That was the only time,
You cold-blooded old thing,
That the ink
Really boiled in your pen.

29

FOOTNOTE TO ST. MATTHEW

Render unto Caesar
The things that are Caesar's,
But you run the risk of
Being called Appeasers.

30

REPLETE ANGLER

A club of fishermen held an outing.
The picnic was planned stag
But one of the anglers brought his new wife.
They spent the day fishing,
The evening lushing,
And the Old Mandarin, with Oriental aplomb,
Sought to relieve the constraint.
He said, to flatter the husband,
"A handsome woman, your wife;
A very fine woman indeed."

The fisherman replied: "You should have seen
The One That Got Away."

ANXIETY

The Old Mandarin was troubled
By a cosmetic advertisement:
COMPACTS GREATLY REDUCED.

The Atlantic Charter?
The Declaration of Moscow?
Teheran?
Quebec?
Yalta?
Potsdam?

OLD MOLE, FAST WORKER

You'll know when youth is definitely fled:
    It's when you turn first to the Obit page.
The chance is, someone whom you knew is dead,
    And, usually, just about your age.

33

Abu Hassan was full of shad:
Every odalisque in Bagdad
Admitted, what it takes, he had.

He used Aleppo
As remount depot.

34

GARDEN IN SPRING

Ye pretty beans that ope your jaws
    Where I do swink and stoop,
I cultivate you, dears, because
    Some day ye shall be soup.

For earthy hands and backbone bent
    Come sprout me, garden gods,
Germination 90%
    And 5½-inch pods.

GARDEN IN AUTUMN

I knew a red October rose that never came to blossom,
    Introverted in the bud, or strictured in the stem;
No sunlight nor solicitude availed it to unbosom—
    There are poems just like that.
                  No one has written them.

Some rust, or frost, or season lost, forbade her curls to
      open;
    Some reluctance in the mind made my communion
      dumb—
But still in secret I review perfections never shapen:
    The rose that could not flower;
                  The word that did not come.

36

*SOFT SHOULDER ON
FIFTH AVENUE*

Confectioners—for instance Schrafft's—
Have the pleasantest of crafts.

Each sweet the candy-merchant wraps
In little crimpy cups. . . . Perhaps

My greedy love likewise belongs
In fluted papers—only songs.

There used to be little golden tongs.

OPERATION EQUATOR

An expanding Mandarin asked the tailor
To let out the waistband of his trousers.
The tailor taped him and was doubtful:
"There ain't enough garment there to give you
All the bulge you need."

"$2\pi r$!" exclaimed the statesman,
"Only 3 inches more girth
Will give almost ½ inch room
All the way round,
Which is true of any circle whatever,
Even the Equator."

Later, musing at ease
In his loosened gear
The Old Mandarin reflected:
If each of the Big Three
Gave way just one inch
We'd have enough slack all round the world
To relieve much global tension.

TRANSLATION FROM
THE CELESTIAL

God was quietly dictating
When He was interrupted.

What was that?

Earth again, said the Angel.
They've discovered an atomic bomb.

Make a note in the tickler file;
We'll check up on that presently.

The stenographic seraph
Poised a golden style. . . .

Those boys better learn
To make friends with themselves:
This time they've really
Scratched the surface.

DON'T FENCE THEM IN

My old sweet stupid spaniel bitch
Shut in her spacious pen
Lies patiently at the gate
Gazing through the wire
Unanimous to be out.

One day, to fell a tree,
The fence at the back of the pen was taken down.
Behind the pooch her world was open wide,
And still she lay frustrated at the gate
Yearning to get free.

It might be risible—if it were not
As poochlike as poor international man
Who never will escape the pen of power
Through the gate of rival sovereignties.
Rover, look round. Behind you the world's open.

HAIR OF THE DOG

Mu Kow always said, before breakfast,
I'll never take another drink,
But he was quite resigned
By lunch time
To prove himself a liar.

REBUKE

I was much annoyed
(Said counsellor Chow Mein)
When your young friend How Kum
Said he dreamed about you.

What impertinence!
If dreams are permitted
I can tell you some beauties.

Lychee nuts! exclaimed Poo Pitty Sing,
A dim view of both of you!
I don't wish to be part
Of anyone's nightmares.

BUT THEY NEVER DID

No celebrity
Has ever discovered
The Midtown Celebrity Bar
But there the Old Mandarin
Had one of his Moments.

Lend me a nickel, he said;
This is the only place I know
Where it costs money
To get into the Wash Room.

Goodness, said Poo Pitty Sing,
His worshipping pupil:
They should pay *You*
To Go.

PROFESSIONAL ZEAL

How I look forward to Wednesday night,
Exclaimed the medical student;
I can hardly wait!

Dear me, wondered the Old Mandarin,
What is it? A fraternity dance?
A basketball game? A beer party?

No indeed, said the student,
His eyes bright with zeal.
For the first time we're going to have
A Fresh Body to dissect.

44

NATURE'S GENTLEWOMAN

What became of your hardy pioneers?
In the foyer of the Gooseberry Room
I was appalled to see
A dulcet young man
Who, while greeting his Girl Friend,
Blandly combed his hair.

45

CHANCELLOR MU KOW'S
ORDER OF THE DAY

Will History repeat?
I got the answer complete
From a man in my street
    With a female pup:

Nations in heat
    Must be kept locked up.

46

THE TOP OF THE MIND

When does Truth come closest?
When you say your thoughts unprocessed.

47

THE VERY TEMPLE

This is the peak of Now,
The very instant when
What you couldn't guess beforehand
Changes to memory
And mercifully improves.

You will not learn in schools
Now is the sharpest of edged tools.

48

THEIR TITLES TAKE

Twenty years ago, two books
Stood accidentally side by side
On an editor's shelf.

I said to him then,
"I hope that's not an omen."
But it was. Those two titles
Were a History of our time.

The books?
The U. S. in Foreign Affairs, and
Funeral Costs.

POETRY IN THE BAG

When I travel I always take with me
Some little anthology of verse.
Usually I don't read it
But just to have it in my bag
Gives the mind a sensitive alert
And I think some of my own.

BOSTON AND MAINE

(TRANSLATION FROM DOWN EAST)

The train want hear the crossin' gong,
    She comes a-bellerin' and a-hissin',
So folks that counts on livin' long
    Stop, Look, and Listen.

TO CERTAIN EDITORS

I also often err
    (My standards are not high)
But never say *infer*
    When I mean *imply*.

What's furthermore, old pals,
    I hope, but daren't expect,
You'll get your *wills* and *shalls*
    Somewhere near correct.

BRIEF BIOGRAPHIES

1

He was a delicious companion
Said Lady Lotus:
He was thoughtful not to say
Things Better Unsaid,
But he always wrote them to me afterward
When I could really enjoy them.

2

Some people said
He was at his best when alone
But he was never like that
When I was with him.

HISTORY OF FICTION

How much untruth
(Said the Chinese novelist)
Must I put in my story
So it will be true
For everybody?

TOO LITERARY

The Old Mandarin learned
His English from dictionaries
And sometimes puzzled
His charming pupils.

"Is it hot enough for you?"
Asked Poo Pitty Sing,
And he answered,
"I'm simply torrefied."

NOTE IN A GIDEON BIBLE

I can't help thinking
That the Jezebel Jewelry Company
On West 47 Street
Have forgotten their Old Testament
Or else been carried away
By alliteration.

IRREVERENCE

Listen! (exclaimed the guests,
Taking tea in the next room)
Listen to the Old Mandarin's typewriter!
He must be going good.

Cumquats, said Poo Pitty Sing.
When he goes as fast as that
He's only X-ing out.

MERIDIONALE

The most perfect lunchtime poem
Is in Muirhead's *Guide to Southern France*
(Macmillan, 1926):—

In Provence, the midday meal
Should be served in a darkened room
And followed by
A siesta.

58

STET!

Poo Pitty Sing wept
In proofreading class.
Such a small mistake, she pleaded.

The Professor of Typography was stern.
Suppose, he said, in 1776
The printer had dropped just one letter,
The Declaration of Independence would read:
When in the curse of human events . . .

Quite right too, she moaned.

59

"Gosh, O.M., I like your stuff so much
I always feel as though
I'd written it myself.
In fact, in the right company,
I use it like original."

I always knew, said the O.M.,
Some day I'd come
Into Someone Else's Own.

60

FLASH!

Po Lil Chile and Young Hyson
Worked on newspaper clip-desks
1000 miles apart
But what a thrill when their letters crossed
And each had sent the other
The same esoteric item
From the Des Moines *Register-Tribune*
Or the Milwaukee *Sentinel.*

CONSOLATION FOR COMMUTERS

Michel de Montaigne
Wouldn't mind if he missed a train.
He'd simply say, Oh hell,
The next one will do just as well.

62

ZENOBIA

Queen Zenobia
Had a touch of xenophobia:
She said, "A murrain
On everything foreign."

THREE-STAR, WOULD
I WERE STEADFAST

I heard him let his hair down in the bar;
He needed to, perhaps, for his morale:

"Listen, Babe, and I'm not jocular,
I'm through with corny fiction—it's banal—
And Lesbian best-sellers. Gal meets gal!
I'm a poet really."

            "Sweet, you *are!*"

"I'd like to write, stead . . . steadfast as a star
One sempiternal sonnet. (Oop.) I shall."

"We better eat."

            "Why spoil it? Two more brandies.
Gosh you're good to talk to." And by now
Beneath the counter they were playing handies.
He eructated, and excused himself.
Meanwhile, O steadfast sonnet, where art thou?

Still shining, in a bottle, on the shelf.

64

A HUSBAND FOR TWO BITS

There's a bookstall in the lobby
(Said Liu-Ti Pie)
And while I was waiting for Captain Much Yen
I bought a Pocket Cook Book
And sat happily reading.

Quite a while later, he said
"I bet you're the only gal
Who ever took a Cook Book
Out to a Dinner Date."

If the Captain is smart,
Said the O.M.,
He'll propose marriage at once.

DIARY UNKEPT

If I lived in a priory
I'd have time to keep a diary
And maliciously quote
Things that get my goat:—

"None of the persons involved in the shooting
Were—as some papers had reported—
Socially prominent."
                    —*New York World-Telegram*

Says the Chinese actuary:
Statistics vary,
But my death by homicide is not imminent
Because I am not Socially Prominent.

66

IGNITION

When you think of a thing
(Said a poet, tall with glory,
Which is very good for poets)
The work is over.
I know what he meant. . . .
I wish it were so.

HISTORY OF OUR TIME?

The artist was in zeal to paint a picture
Before contractors bulldozed through the hill
And shattered the old barn.

Leftward of his easel
Approached the grinding uproar and the clamor
Of concrete mixer and pile driver.

When he got home, examining his canvas,
The left side of the sketch
Was thin and blank, unbalanced.
How, he wondered then, had he been pleased
With a study so ill-composed?

What he had thought to be
Part of the picture
Was, in fact, only Noise.

THROUGH TRAIN

Softly, softly, a train can go
When the track is padded with snow.

Then, without echo and rattle and jar,
The daycoach rides like a Pullman car.

One snowy day I almost caught
The Limited Train—a train of thought.

FAMILY WEEK-END

Posterity is pushing me hard:
I can't go out the front door
Because robins are nesting in the hinge;
I can't go through the side-porch
Because the puppy is taking her nap.
I can't paint epigrams
Because Po Chile is using my brush;
I can't turn on the radio
For some wonderful folksy commercials
Because Pal Jo is reading Thomas Aquinas
And Poo Pitty Sing
Is sleeping off a hangover.

LOW MEMORABILITY

What sort of a day, O.M.?

Wonderful!
I thought of the absolutely right word
For one of my little sayings.
So right that no one
Will ever notice it.

Good old rainbow-chaser!
What was it?

Sacro-iliac! . . . I've forgotten.

SYMPTOM

The Old Mandarin blew his friends
Mr. and Mrs. Yung Wed
To a tenderloin dinner.
How about a bottle of Bass?

Oh swell! cried Mrs. Yung,
The very thing I want;
Exactly what I've been craving,
I'm ca-razy for bitter ale!
And largesse of red gravy!
Her eyes bigged and brightened and glistened
And her brow grew damp with desire.

The benevolent old behaviorist
Nudged Mr. Yung, and whispered:
Congratulations! I see
You're going to have a baby.

The apprentice husband was furious.
"Confucius!" he exclaimed,
"I only learned it last night myself.
How did *you* know?"

He has been suspicious
Ever since.

WARNING

Said Clemenceau, that old French realist,
War is too serious
To be managed
By the generals alone.

True also of education,
Which is much too important
To be left only in the hands
Of teachers.

73

EPICURI DE GREGE

(HORACE: *Epistles* I, iv, 16)

The Old Mandarin complained
Of a stye on his eye.
I wonder, he asked,
Could it come from drinking?
An Epicurean stye, as Horace said?

Not a bit of it, said the tactful barkeep;
That's what you get when you're run down.
It comes from working too hard.

Why is it only bartenders tell you
What you most want to hear?

FILE AND FORGET

The publisher asked for a blurb
About his new volume
And was grieved when I wrote
*This is a book I'd be proud to have
On the bookseller's shelves.*

"A CHILL NO COAT"

Comes the Season of Silence:
The Old Mandarin resumes his gown of hodden gray
And wary as a mouse in a woodbasket
Draws in for the winter.

He puts his wax ear-stopples near the hearth
(They'll be soft to plug in when needed).
The hurricane gave him plenty of firewood,
Publishers give him enough to read
And the radio more than enough
To meditate.

Blessing, to stay for a while in One Place;
Not have to go Anywhere;
Nowhere at all.

Like the draught from a leaking window
Comes a gooseflesh thought:
Eventually, O.M.,
You must.

MERCY STROKE

I am just sat down for lunch
When Mrs. Soft Heart next door
Comes me weeping in
With a sorely wounded robin.
"Poor thing, it was hurt by the cat.
Kill it for me, please, I simply can't."

It was warm and light in my hand
While I hunted for the axe
Which weighed extra heavy.
I measured for mercy stroke.
The mangled bird, precious to itself,
Saw the great edge poised,
Screamed a dreadful croak,
Looked me through and through
With damnation of the world.

Sickened, I cast away
(And twice; and heavy now)
The ruined flying thing
In its own forgetful thicket.
There is still a little stain
On the fresh white hurricane stump.

Lunch was not a success.

CHINESE BARTLETT

They asked the Old Mandarin:
Why don't you write a real book,
Something with less promiscuity
And more continuity?

He replied: What remains of any book
After a little while
But a few quotes and excerpts?
A few half-rememberables
More than half-forgotten.*
Why not just write the excerpts
To begin with?

* Half-remembered is not the same
  As half-forgotten.
  The half we remembered
  Is *ours*.

GOOD REASON

Churchill quoted Clough,
F.D.R. quoted Longfellow,
Truman quoted Tennyson.
Maybe the Victorians
Aren't so dead after all.
And I'm getting nearly old enough
To be quoted myself.

Oh no, said the Mandarin,
When things are really serious
They don't quote a living poet
Because he'd never
Stop talking about it.

A HAPPY DAY

He trimmed his garden
And pruned his epigrams,
Each task, he hoped,
Improved by the other.
He went happily to and fro
Between poems and peonies,
Aphids and aphorisms.

A musician must baby his hands,
But earthy nails never spoiled a poet.

CLASS IN CREATIVE WRITING

The unrecognized poet
Has glorious relish
In contemplating his own verse.
He knows how few others
Ever will.

Pray always to remain
An unrecognized poet.
Besides, this is a prayer
Not unlikely to be fulfilled.

ARE YOU THERE?

A poor old Mandarin
Sat alone:
The bell kept trilling,
Phone . . . phone . . . phone . . .

He answered unwilling,
Reluctant, loth;
First with a moan,
Then with an oath.

Who passed around the word, the jerk,
That today I was trying to do some work.

IN CASE OF FIRE

The true artist
In any art
Never admits visitors
Behind the scenes.
When you're putting on an act
The only spectator allowed backstage
Is the Fireman.

PRECAUTION

The Conservator in Chungking
Asked them to save all paper,
Use it again and again.

Stop! the Old Mandarin cried to his houseboy
Who was packing a parcel
To mail to the Duchess.
Better not use that paper,
It came from a Different Dame;
Her name and address are on it.

O Master of Tact, exclaimed Gin Rickshaw:
We better file wrapping paper, too.

84

MYTHOLOGY

Zeus
Was either abstruse
Or else on the loose.
He was grand to do Leda-and-the-Swan with
But other times he was hard to get on with.

Most of that Olympic set
Were hail fellows well unmet.

85

INSTRUCTIONS FOR A
SOCIAL SECRETARY

A man who works at a desk
Can sometimes get to be *Esq.*

If their jobs involve blisters
They're only Misters.

CHINK IN HIS ARMOR

He was known as a Great Reader
But could never force himself to peruse
The sinister clauses
Of very small type
In an insurance policy.

PHILOLOGIST AT THE TRAIN GATE

Have they no vowels of compassion?
  By some Grimm Law they always say
In their peculiar diphthong fashion:
  ALL ABARD FOR ERSTER BAY!

This idiosyncrasy should teach
Some new phonetic law of speech,
But never mind linguistic turns—
We'll miss it! Hurry! GOID YOUR LERNS!

CHINESE MOTHER GOOSE

Windy Kate, Windy Kate,
Nothing can vindicate.
Once she was only a newspaper syndicate.

But worse came later:
As Commentator
Thoughts the banalest
Speech the flannelest
Accent infernalest.

No longer journalist
Now she's an Analyst.

89

REVISION

Life is so strangely misshapen:
>   If I had a chance to correct it,
Sometimes I'd let something happen
>   When I Most expect it.

90

POSTSCRIPT

There's still a little meaning left
In some of these verses,
Like toothpaste in a tube.
But squeeze it out flat—
Don't twist it

PERPLEXITIES OF A POET

The poet, Young Hyson, asked himself
About his new lyric:
Do I feel strongly enough
For hard, unchangeable type?
Suppose it were only true
On Mondays, Wednesdays, Fridays?

Alas, that print has no
Frequency Modulation.

DEVOTION

Asked Poo Pitty Sing, his admiring pupil:
Are you going to write a poem today?

I don't think so, my dear;
I'm not relaxed enough.

Goodness, she murmured, if that's all . . .

Next spring he was among
The Publishers' Announcements.

93

CLASS DISMISSED

One of his lovely pupils
Studying Chinese classics
Said, "It occurs to me,
What is the feminine for *Mandarin?*"

"It occurs to me,"
Said the Old Mandarin gallantly,
"*You* are."

DIM VIEW

"I've been reading," said Poo Pitty Sing,
"The *Journal to Stella*.
Gosh, what letters
The Dean did write her;
But I take rather
A dim view of Stella:
What did she have
That **I** haven't got?"

She had Jonathan Swift.

FOR A MOOD TOO PSYCHOPATH
HIS DOCTOR ORDERS A HOT BATH

Sink your tingling dorsal in
This reservoir of porcelain.

For your complaint a steaming wallow
Beats all other physic hollow.

Just relax, and growing pink
Don't allow yourself to think.

Lie there till the water's tepid
And your humor grows more lepid.

Soap and silence be your drug.
Perfect in vacuity,
Tell your mind: *Now let me be!*
Then pull the plug.

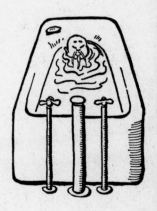

FORWARDED

During the years underground
I wrote many letters to Marianne
(The spirit of France).

Sometimes she was away
But they were all marked
Faites suivre, s.v.p.

NOTE FOR A BRITISH TRAVELER

Across our flat Long Island shires
You need not look for huntsman squires.
That barking is not hounds or harriers,
But caused by (Y*oicks!*) hay-fever carriers.

COEFFICIENT OF CREDIBILITY

We turned on the radio
In the middle of a program.
The news from abroad was really terrific
But I noticed the Old Mandarin
Wasn't paying attention.
"I'm waiting to hear who the sponsor is.
How can I guess how much to believe
Unless I know what they're advertising?"

BIOGRAPHY OF KING CANUTE

In the best Mongolian manner
Was a phrase I noticed once
In the *Saturday Evening Post:*
"The Future
And How to Prevent It."

BREAKFAST SPOILED

Bill Chung was enraged
By the inexpert waitress.
He gazed rigid as a pointer
While she fussed and fiddled in serving
Till the eggs were dour
And the coffee cold.
Peevishly he asked, "What tip shall I give her?"

Poor wench, pleaded the placable Mandarin,
She's only dumb; she was trying her best.

"You're making me soft!" cried Chung,
Adding a nickel.

IT ISN'T EVEN FUNNY

I have a special feeling (said Big Eyes)
About the last match in the folder.
I save it with prudence,
I strike it carefully,
With queer emotion
Which I can't define.
Is it feminine thrift?

No, my dear, it is a true instinct
To make ceremonial
Of casual moments.
The Last of anything
Is always sacred.

ANGUISH IN HERBA

The friendly curious children
    Loquaciously come near:
The poet in his greenwood
    Lurks in angry fear.

There, his private thinking
    By innocence defiled,
More than hell or Hitler
    He fears the neighbor's child.

ETHICAL CULTURE

One of my favorite Mandarins
(In fact, Mr. Simeon Strunsky)
Passing through the mellay of Times Square
Sees at the door of a vast building
A sign that sends him to work
In a glow of tranquil cheer:—
SHINE INSIDE.

WHERE THE WASTE BEGINS

Wonderful wasteful wacky America!
When the carpenters built my seaside pagoda
They threw away so many chips and chunks,
Planks and wedges of useful lumber
That three years later
I'm still using them
To kindle fires.

Your mind, O.M., was like that too.

105

JURY RIG

Patiently, said the Old Mandarin,
I accustomed myself to zippers,
But one evening I had to wear
My pre-war dinner suit.
Just one unconscious gesture
And a whole row of confidential buttons
Pattered on the tiles.

I had to go to His Excellency's party
Toggled together
With matchsticks.

INVESTIGATION OF THE
ALCOHOLIC BEVERAGE INDUSTRY

Although it costs at least a fin
They do not dare to call it *gin*.
All of Geneva it inherits
Is the label: Neutral Spirits.

"AUTHOR WILL SUPPLY"

The anxious author, when engaged
Correcting proof sheets newly paged
May find a memo of this sort
(The printer's warning): ONE LINE SHORT.

And though I write this verse of mine
  To give your thought a moment's play,
The text is also short one line—
  And you know well what it would say.

APOLOGY TO NEIGHBORS
FOR LOOKING SO IDLE

The poet, on his verse intent,
    Or the artist, dreaming paint,
Probably look indolent—
    But they ain't.

STEPPING OUT

The neighbors were rattled when the O.M.,
Usually unsociable,
Walked round one evening
To pay a call.
"To what, if one may ask,
Do we owe this pleasure?"

"It was just the right distance
To break in my new pair of shoes."

DOWAGER AT LARGE

We had been talking
Of our dignified friend the Dowager
And her painful arthritis,
But the conversation switched
And His Excellency, who is very deaf,
Did not realize the topic was now
The ancient steamer *Lady of the Lake*.

"She doesn't go out much now," I shouted,
"Only an occasional excursion,
But I saw her come backing in.
Old sweetheart, she whistled for the buoys,
Waving her walking beam she turned on one paddle
And coasted sideways on her flat bottom.
I threw her a line myself."

"What?" cried His Excellency. "The Dowager? You hor-
rify me!"

PRACTICAL ARTIST

Shrewd aphorist was that sculptor
Who used to mould pictures in sand
On the beach at Atlantic City.
Beside his display was the sign:
To Praise I'm Deferential
But the Coins are the Essential.

BAKER STREET EXERCISE

It's often interesting
To walk round someone's property
And try to deduce
What sort of person lives there
But it takes courage to do it
Round one's own.

SENS UNIQUE

"Avenue des cyprès qui va de l'utérus au sépulcre."
—*Inédits de Leon Bloy*

In *sens unique* (to wit, one-way)
    The traffic moves for travelers whom
Our sombre Avenue des Cyprès
    Conducts from uterus to tomb.

114

Sometimes . . . not always . . .
When the telephone rings
He says, Don't they know
The mails are working?

Sometimes . . . not always . . .
When he gets a letter
He asks, Have they heard
That there are postcards?

Postcards are written
By strong happy people.
Trouble takes more
Than a one-cent stamp.

EASY WISDOM

Poison ivy had no fears
Till gardeners came with gloves and shears.

The tourist thought the road a cinch
Till caught without a monkey wrench.

The Girl Scouts didn't know what damp meant
Till they went out on encampment. . . .

Then I cried: *Mot de Cambronne!*
Leave these to oblivion!

You can learn on any shelves
    It's easy to be wise in rhyme:
    Choosing their own mood and time
Men write when they're by themselves.
The poets and the aphorists
Are the true isolationists.

LIFE BEGINS AT X

Poo Pitty Sing
Was beginning algebra;
Her instructor strove
To arouse her mind.

"If I'm 25 years older than you,
When will you be
Two-thirds my age?"

She didn't even need
An equation with x's:
"Never!" she cried gaily,
"You know damn well
You won't live that long."

He was sorry he asked.
Teachers of mathematics
Age rapidly.

117

VALEDICTORIAN

Of Death, as of Life,
Perhaps we will say
I wouldn't have missed it
For the World.

MONGOLIAN PROVERBS

Who tunes in late, escapes the Sponsor.

An author's highest ambition: to be a Bathroom Book.

He was a Model Pupil—funny, I can't remember his
name.

AN EPITAPH: He was always where the thinking was
thickest.

HISTORY: From cave man to bomb cave in 3000 genera-
tions.

DIALOGUE

—I shouldn't have spent so much time carving cherrystones.
—Those weren't cherrystones. They were millstones.

LAST ADVICE

So you won't need to cancel
 The thoughts that you really think,
Use less indelible pencil
 And more invisible ink.